# Märchen

# Märchen
## The Art of Craig Wetzel

Edited by Madison Wetzel
With essays by Joshua Drake and Princess Rapunzel

Märchen: The Art of Craig Wetzel

This volume has been published in conjunction with the exhibition
*Märchen: The Art of Craig Wetzel,*
hosted by the Ohio Valley Regional Arts Council, April 23 - May 8, 2015,
Kent State University at East Liverpool

ISBN-13: 978-1508489122
ISBN-10: 1508489122

Published by Craig Wetzel's Imaginactory
Designed and edited by Madison Wetzel

Craig Wetzel's Imaginactory
P.O. Box 326 East Liverpool, OH 43920
imaginactory.com

Photography by R. David Pickens & Craig Wetzel
Front and back cover: Craig Wetzel, *Mermaid,* 2012. Egg tempera on panel.

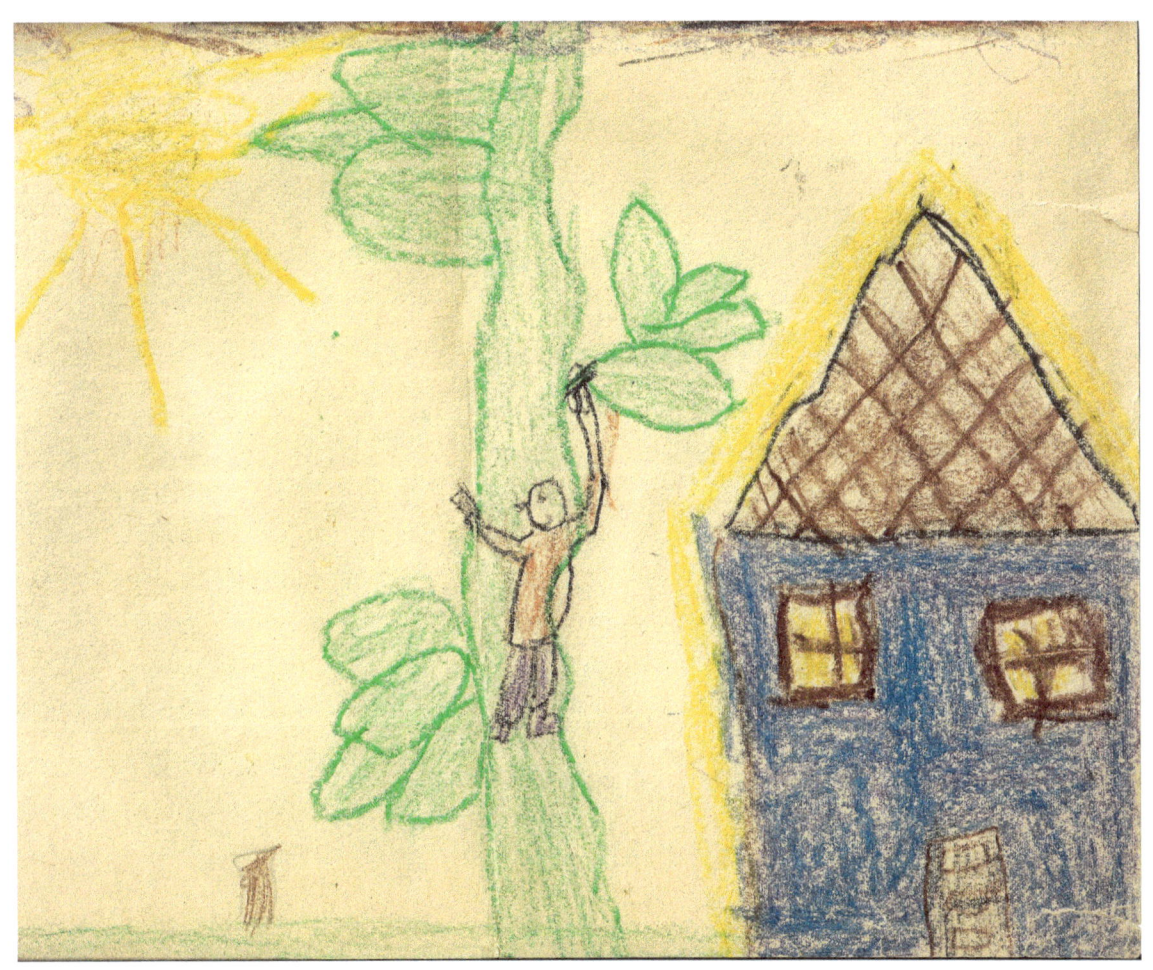

*Jack and the Beanstalk,* 1970

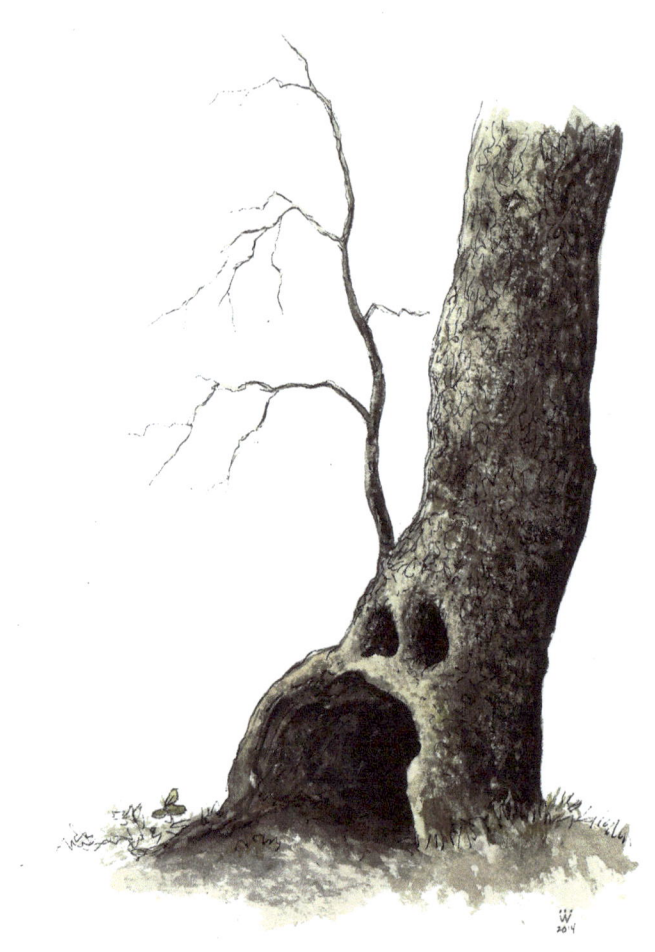

*Anthropomorphic Sycamore, 2014*

# Contents

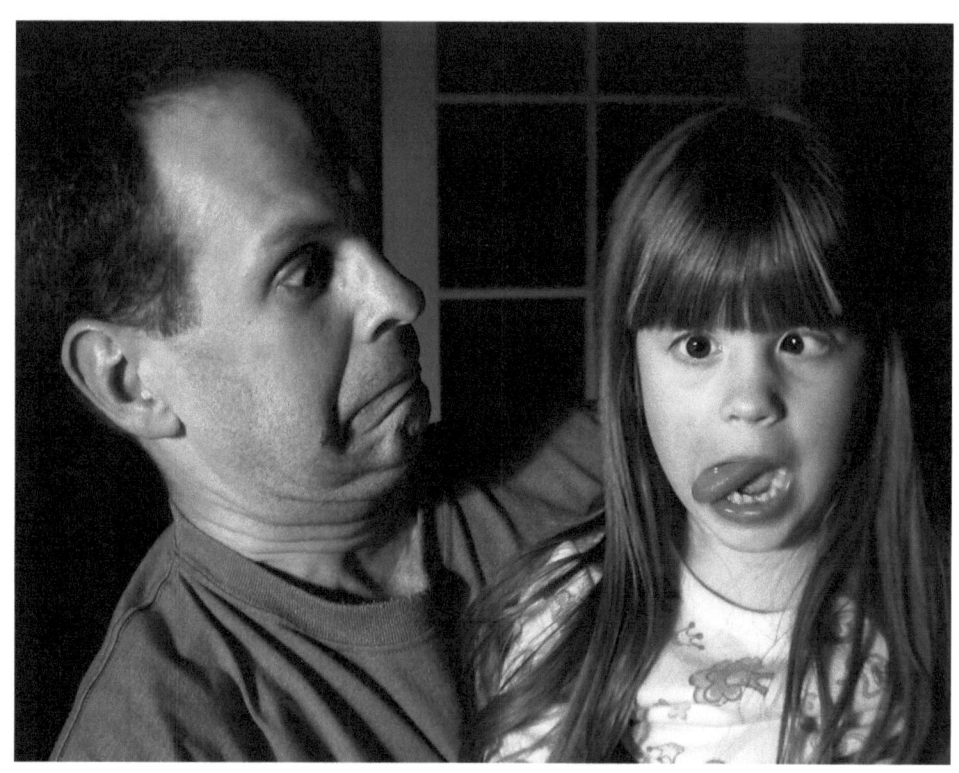

*Craig & Madison, 2002*

# A Note from the Editor

Once upon a time, the Dutch Post-Impressionist painter Vincent Van Gogh wrote, "Paintings have a life of their own that derives from the painter's soul." The art of my father, Craig Wetzel, provides no better example of the truth in that statement. By simply walking from my bedroom to our kitchen, I have the pleasure of experiencing just a small portion of the imagination that resides in my father's mind. His intense love and interest for what is and what could be radiates from his work. It would be an understatement to say that the creativity in his artwork, as well as his love for art in general, has had a great impact on my life.

When I was young, one of my favorite pastimes was to go to my father's art studio, where I would play whatever music I was interested in at the time and pretend to put on a show. I spent hours in the studio every day, never paying attention to what was around me. Looking back on it, I realize that the place I would go to get lost in my imagination was the place where my father would do the same. I never paid attention to the paint bottles, brushes, easels, pencils, sketches, and half-finished paintings. Because I was so invested in my own imagination, I never took the time to experience his.

In recent years, my father and I have found a new passion in art. At least once a month I beg him to take me to an art museum. We often find ourselves looking through books filled with the art of some of the greatest—Rembrandt, Van Gogh, Andrew Wyeth, Vermeer—the list goes on. We discuss the motives and history behind each work of art. He even asks for my opinion of his own artwork from time to time, no matter how brutal my comments may be. Thanks to him, I have been able to experience a new world, one of creativity and imagination, where the passion and immense love for a combination of reality and dreams is shown with every brushstroke.

Often times, both as children and adults, we spend most of our time inside our own mind, living in our own worlds. We dream about what was and what could be. We imagine a world completely different from the one in which we live. We immerse ourselves in our own daydreams, but we never take the time to look at others'. We are so wrapped up in our own imaginations, that we forget that everyone around us has fantasies as well. They also live in worlds beyond belief and comprehension. What if we could see those worlds? What if, for a short period of time, we stopped living in our world, and visited someone else's?

When I walk into my father's studio now, I take time to look around. I notice the little doodles on random papers. I look at the sketches lying around. I flip through the watercolor books. I take the time to step out of my imagination and into his. For tonight, I invite you to do the same. Leave your imaginary world at the door and step into the world of Craig Wetzel. Experience the magic and fantasy that is *Märchen*.

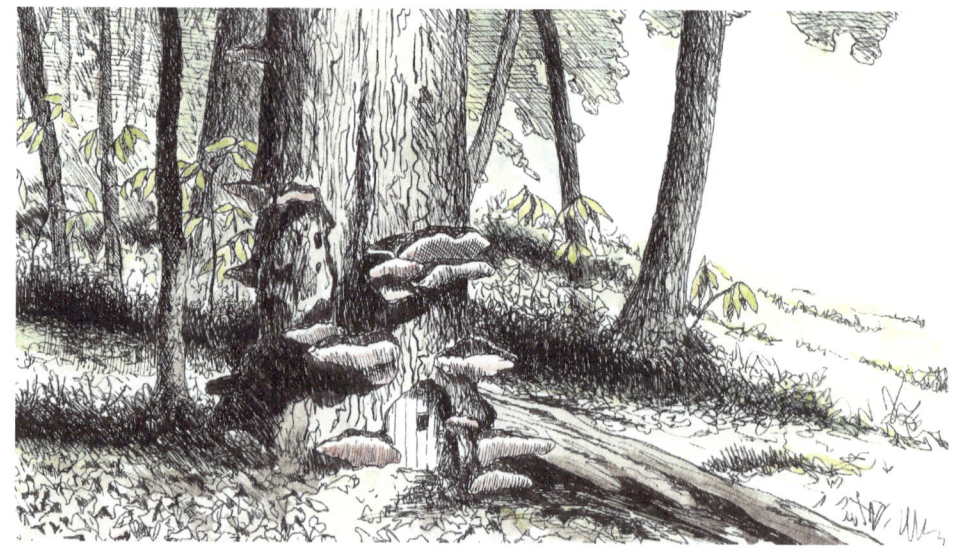

*Home of the Elves,* 2013

# How to Paint in Tempera and Avoid Making Kitsch

Joshua Drake

Giorgio Vasari, the sixteenth-century biographer of the artists of the Italian Renaissance, was obviously an Italian. The first publication of his most famous work, *Lives of the Most Excellent Painters, Sculptors, and Architects,* was printed in 1500 and included only Italians. At the end of his second and expanded edition in 1568, he somewhat begrudgingly turned his attention, at the end of the volume, to 'diverse Flemish artists.' Why he felt thus compelled is demonstrable, however, for he credits the most important of them, Jan van Eyck with unlocking the secrets of oil painting. By 1568, linseed oil had become the most popular medium for painting, rapidly supplanting the older and more taxing medium of egg tempera. While Vasari oversimplifies, his truism that oil painting gained ascendance in Northern Europe to be passed southward, mostly by the hands of Leonardo, is still a convenient generalization of the historic ascendance of oil over eggs. Yet, it must be noticed that, notwithstanding the new medium's popularity, one of Michelangelo's first paintings was in mixed medium. His famous Doni Tondo, with its holy family situated before a background of his characteristically irrelevant casual nude males, is only partly in oil. Many of the fleshy passages were done in egg instead, in spite of the technical problems such a mixed media work would present. Why Michelangelo preferred egg to oil, at least in some instances, is instructive, for in 1507 there seems less and less to commend eggs over oil, unless one is frying breakfast. Oil surely bears more pigment, is mixable, does not dry quickly allowing for easy reworking, needs one brush stroke for every thirty in egg, creates texture, and binds to surfaces more easily. What's not to like? The young Michelangelo knew, and I suspect Craig Wetzel's art itself will demonstrate this. While oil can be used in thin transparent glazes, it is much slower to be used thus because of the very thing that makes it great--its slow dry time. But egg dries almost instantly and allows re-glazing within moments. Consequently, every surface can be easily made a translucent one, built of imperceptibly thin coats of pigment and egg. This lends a warmness and softness that actually approximates most natural objects better, since the surface of most organic objects are themselves translucent--made up of imperceptible layers of thin cells.

Warmness and softness, however, come with their own costs, and especially so in our age. Kitsch art relies on softness of features to lead viewers back into the retreat of their own imaginations, since it forbids the hard objects of real life to take hold on one. Taking the viewer out of both the real world and the world of the artist, these soft surfaces encourage mere glancing rather than careful and contemplative looking. Left in the world of their own imaginations, rather than in this world or one imagined by the artist, the viewers are then allowed to know only what they can themselves bring to the work, rather than learning from the artist and his peculiar gifts of sight and expression. The broad commercial appeal of artists who create these warm and fuzzy images (notice how quickly the adjective 'fuzzy' can be substituted for 'soft' and thus redefine 'warm') has brought them an odium among serious artists, to which these same serious artists sometimes unfortunately react. Wetzel is happily not a reactionary. Neither has he an interest in sentimentalism or commercial success. His egg tempera technique allows the best of the medium without succumbing to the worst of it. He achieves this success in three ways--through pallet, composition, and whimsy.

Wetzel's pallet defies the kitsch artist and the mainstream contemporary artist alike. Wetzel's is an unflinching earthtone. His reliance on earth pigments, spotted rarely with a few manmade primaries, forbids the pastel haze that defines so much commercial kitsch. One cannot here be lured into a false world of glowing lupines and towering Japanese maples that phosphoresce from the surface of the work like the neon signs above a Vegas casino. At the same time, Wetzel avoids a rather infrequently observed problem in some mainstream contemporary art. Some of this art succeeds because it must catch the eyes of a culture seared by back-lit screens and pop-up ads. In an effort to compete, many forms of postmodern art employ the aggressive sight-destroying bombast of various forms of pop culture. Warhol's silk-screen acrylics and Rauschenberg's mock abstract expressionism would see Wetzel's pallet as lacking in sensation. And, frankly, it does lack sensation. It relies on subtlety rather than the aggressive chromaticism of popular marketing. If it fails to gain attention thereby, Wetzel seems to say, 'so much the better.' Every work's color seems to say, 'keep your cadmiums and halogen and enjoy the color of dirt and moss.'

Wetzel's compositions, of all the basic features of his work, surely ask the most patience from the viewer. The approach given to the viewer is rarely a natural one, like the compositions of Sargent, Degas, or Manet. Neither is it contrived according to convention like Raphael, David, or Ingres. His compositions haven't careless spontaneity nor have they studied fastidiousness. But they do work, as anyone will know who spends time with them. They work, if for no other reason than that they are neither careless nor conventional. 'What would it be like,' Wetzel seems to say, 'if we were to see the world as it would be if our eyes prioritized the objects we liked the most and thrust them forward a bit, moved them to the fore a bit more, or tilted the plane of vision so that they were more emphatic.' It seems, at least in my view, that he has a hieratic approach to composition, like the early icon-painters, only instead of making the holiest saint larger or more emphatic, he makes the ugliest tree or the most misshapen rock larger or more emphatic. This hallowed object is then placed off-center, not according to the natural rules of objective design that say symmetrical compositions are flat, but according to the spiritual rules that say that the holiest objects cannot be addressed directly. It is almost as if Wetzel can't quite center the thing he loves the most for fear that it would be too rich and too intense for us to take.

This reverence doesn't last long, however. Almost as if he discovers this holy and reverential seriousness to be distasteful, Wetzel then usually turns to laughter. After painting a set of rocks so painstakingly, or delighting us all in the beauty of some gnarly old oak, he smiles and inserts a pig or a broken baby doll or a pair of feet or a smiling crow or some other inexplicability. One is tempted almost to anger at the sight of these objects. Why mar such a lovely scene with such nonsense? A moment's reflection will discover the necessity of it all. The effect is of someone who is taking himself pretty seriously and then catches himself in the idolatrous mistake of it all. Who has not been taken in by a full moon and been tempted not only to draw or paint her, but actually to worship? Anyone who really loves art almost certainly has had something of this experience unless he is infected by *Der Stijl*. Wetzel helps us to discover our temptation to 19th century pantheism. He puts our proper delight in nature in its rightful restraint—nature has her charms but she is no true goddess. Indeed, she is more like a nymph. And when we worship her as the Romantics did, without Wetzel's jokes to interrupt us, we end in their desperation.

If Vasari were to come back from the dead, he would not likely re-edit his book to include a new chapter on the 'diverse Ohio Artists.' But if he were induced to do so, he would talk about Wetzel in similar terms to Van Eyck, only in inversion. 'He rediscovered the secrets of painting with egg and defied his whole age in doing so.' Vasari would probably have many enchanting things to tell us about Wetzel's life as well, but those delicacies are not a matter for this critic to disclose.

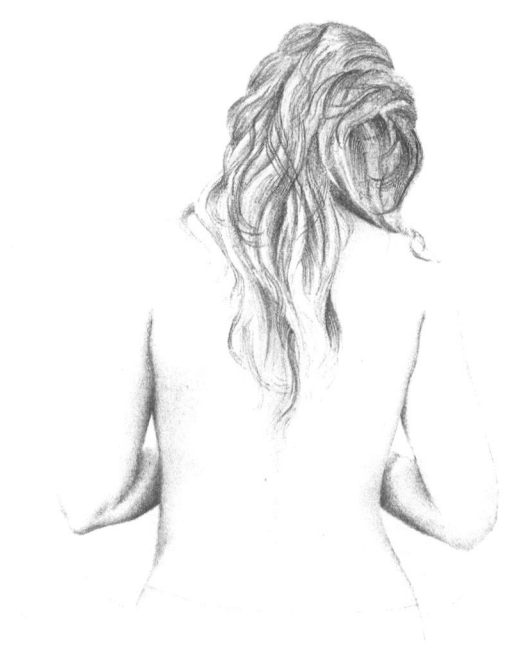

*Mermaid* (study), 2012

# A View from the Tower

Princess Rapunzel

The innocence of my youth is too familiar to bear repeating for its own sake. Indeed, innocence is the norm for those of us who have lived our formative years in the magical world of *märchen*. And yet my youth and inexperience were unique even within the realm of fairy tales, and as my subsequent appreciation of the visual arts was influenced, in large part, by the absence of beauty in my early life, some of my history, although piper's news, may bear repeating.

From my earliest memory, I had known no other than the wicked witch. I had felt no mother's caress, had heard not the kind words of a father, and had no friend with whom to share my thoughts save the birds who lighted each morning on my casement. Of physical needs I wanted nothing. For the improvement of my mind the witch, though not from any kindness on her part, had furnished my solitary room with a well-chosen library, the pleasure of which, knowing nothing of the world beyond my tower, was "dukedom large enough." It was with these books, solaces beyond measure, that I spent my days, delighting in a life I was certain I would never know, little considering that such places and people might exist outside of the walls within which I dwelt.

If my imprisonment had kept me from beauty, my banishment subsequent to the discovery of my pregnancy would show me nothing but the ugliness of the world. But as I surveyed the barren wasteland of my home each day, I felt that both myself and the prince's two children were destined to know greater things than imprisonment in towers or exile in desert places. Without being able to articulate the thought, I knew that I was part of a fairy tale. Because of that belief, I determined to remain hopeful, knowing that good would prevail and that I, like so many *märchenvolks* before me, would live happily ever after, that true love would reign despite the trials I had yet to endure.

Upon my reuniting with the prince and the restoration of his sight, you may imagine with what feelings of joy and rapture we entered his kingdom as husband and wife. The verdant shades, bucolic scenes, rocky crags, and crystal brooks that met my view as we entered this fair land, often denigrated by scholars of our lives as clichès, were as fresh and new to me as the grass upon which I would often fall, overwhelmed by happiness, shedding tears of unspeakable joy. Those who have not been incarcerated in a phallic symbol by an evil witch simply have no idea of the beauty that surrounds them.

It was not long after I had settled into the castle as a new bride that I first became aware of the art of Mr. Wetzel. My good friend Snow White stopped by one afternoon with a house-warming gift of fresh-picked rampions and our conversation turned to the redecoration of a wing in her castle, specifically to a painting that she had recently purchased, sight unseen, on the strong recommendation of a discerning dealer of fine art. Although the art collection of which she was now the curator had been started many years ago by the wicked queen, it had been neglected in the last years of her reign. As the queen's hatred for Snow White consumed her, a disdain for all beauty naturally followed, until her only thought was to one day dine on the internal organs of my companion, foregoing all interest in the arts and the finer things of our world. After the queen's fortunate death and my dear friend's subsequent return to the home of her youth, Snow began supplementing the queen's collection with occasional purchases, thereby feeding a enthusiasm for paintings that had, of necessity, lain dormant during her exile with the dwarves, an enthusiasm that has continued unabated to this day and a passion that, from my first sight of her magnificent collection, we have shared and that has been our strongest bond.

As we enjoyed the rampions that day, Snow mentioned the latest addition to her collection, already selected to be the centerpiece of the newly decorated wing. So strongly did she lavish praise upon her "newest discovery", so unreserved was her admiration of the artist, that I could hardly forego waiting until the next day to see it.

I arose at day-spring the following morning and, accompanied by my retinue, set off for the castle with feelings of delightful anticipation. Upon being shown into the gallery in which the painting had been temporarily installed, I was immediately thunderstruck, standing in rapturous awe at the portrait of our mutual friend, Briar Rose, as she had appeared at the time of the unfortunate incident with the spinning wheel [included in this exhibit]. Despite Snow's insistence that the painting was unenchanted, I could hardly believe the artist had not used a magic brush. With tears in my eyes, I determined that I must own one of the artist's works for our castle. My husband and I now own three of Mr. Wetzel's paintings and they are the highlights of what is, I am proud to say, one of the finest collections in the kingdom, perhaps second only to that of my dear friend, Snow.

Although we had corresponded several times, I had yet to meet Mr. Wetzel when I was delighted one day to receive a note saying that he was in the neighborhood of the castle and wished to offer his regards. So excited was I to meet the man who had, in a short time, become my favorite artist, that I forsook all propriety and ran to the moat, where I welcomed him like a dansey-headed schoolgirl meeting a knight. His greeting, though polite, showed none of the warmth I expected and as our conversation was interrupted by several uncomfortable pauses, I necessarily guided our talk towards his interests. Once upon a subject with which he was familiar, he became passionate in his conversation, forgetting his natural reticence. As the guards marched around the castle and the swans swam lazily in the moat, Mr. Wetzel and I sat on the parapet and talked of many wonderful things, not realizing how much time had passed until we were surprised by the alarm that precedes the raising of the drawbridge at eventide. It now being too late for the gentleman to consider traveling further, Mr. Wetzel acceded to my entreaties that he be a guest of the prince and me for the night.

The prince returned soon after dark from hunting in the great forest and we enjoyed a delightful feast of roasted goblin, fresh rampion salad, stuffed rabblefish, and mead. Although I had anticipated inquiring further as to Mr. Wetzel's views on the arts, my dear husband, upon discovering Mr. Wetzel's love of casting an angle, would talk of nothing else but fins and feathers. Still, Mr. Wetzel's unusual sense of humor was such a delight that it was nearly dawn when we bid our guest good night and retired to bed. In the three years that have since passed, I have had ample time to probe his inner thoughts on painting, poetry, literature, and a myriad of other subjects that interest him, and I have come to love Mr. Wetzel as one of my dearest friends.

Although he enjoys working with both pen & ink and watercolors, he prefers egg tempera, an ancient medium even by fairy tale standards, enjoying the slow, laborious work of adding thousands of brush strokes to build an image to his satisfaction. I might also add that he has often said, albeit somewhat facetiously, that he prizes the eggs of our chickens above all others for mixing his paint.

He is known throughout the kingdoms as a great lover of the forest. Many times have I come upon him, sketch box at his side, working intently in some shady glen or beside a sparkling stream, plying the trade for which he seems most temperamentally suited. Nor does he confine himself to the beautiful things, having painted such evil and malignant creatures as woodwives, elves, and trolls. When discussing his art, he often projects an indifference that is somewhat disturbing to the uninitiated. It is commonly known that once a painting is completed, he has little interest in it, not caring whether it hangs in the hall of a great castle or languishes in the barn of a peasant, his only interest being directed to whatever work is in progress. Though no misanthrope, he avoids people in groups, which he defines as "anyone and someone else," preferring the company of his books and his thoughts to all others.

He thinks little of his work, believing that painting is of small importance to the world. He insists, despite evidence to the contrary, that his natural talents are limited; that only through sustained application and hard work has he reached a level of accomplishment that he believes to be little more than mediocre. It is not generally known that he intends to give up painting altogether, having fallen into the craft "by accident," and after nearly three decades of toil, "is thoroughly sick of it". As Mr. Wetzel remains enigmatic and unpredictable even to those who know him best, it is difficult to say whether his imagination will travel in a new direction or if, having had time to feel the absence of a craft he has pursued for thirty years, he will, on some future day, break some eggs, pull a brush from a jar, and attack his art with renewed interest.

It is my dearest hope that you will enjoy these paintings as I have. Many of the scenes you will see are from my kingdom, the people you will meet among my dearest friends. Keep reading fairy tales!

*Adapted from a speech given at the 2014 Annual Meeting of Märchenvolks, Le Château de Cendrillon, France.*

NOTE: It is with great reluctance that my husband and I have agreed to put several paintings on the market. Were it not for the troublesome infestation of elves in the castle, we would never have agreed to part with any of our paintings, but the egg tempera with which Mr. Wetzel uses being particularly tasteful to the evil creatures, we have no option but to sell, if only to preserve them for future generations.

The Exhibition

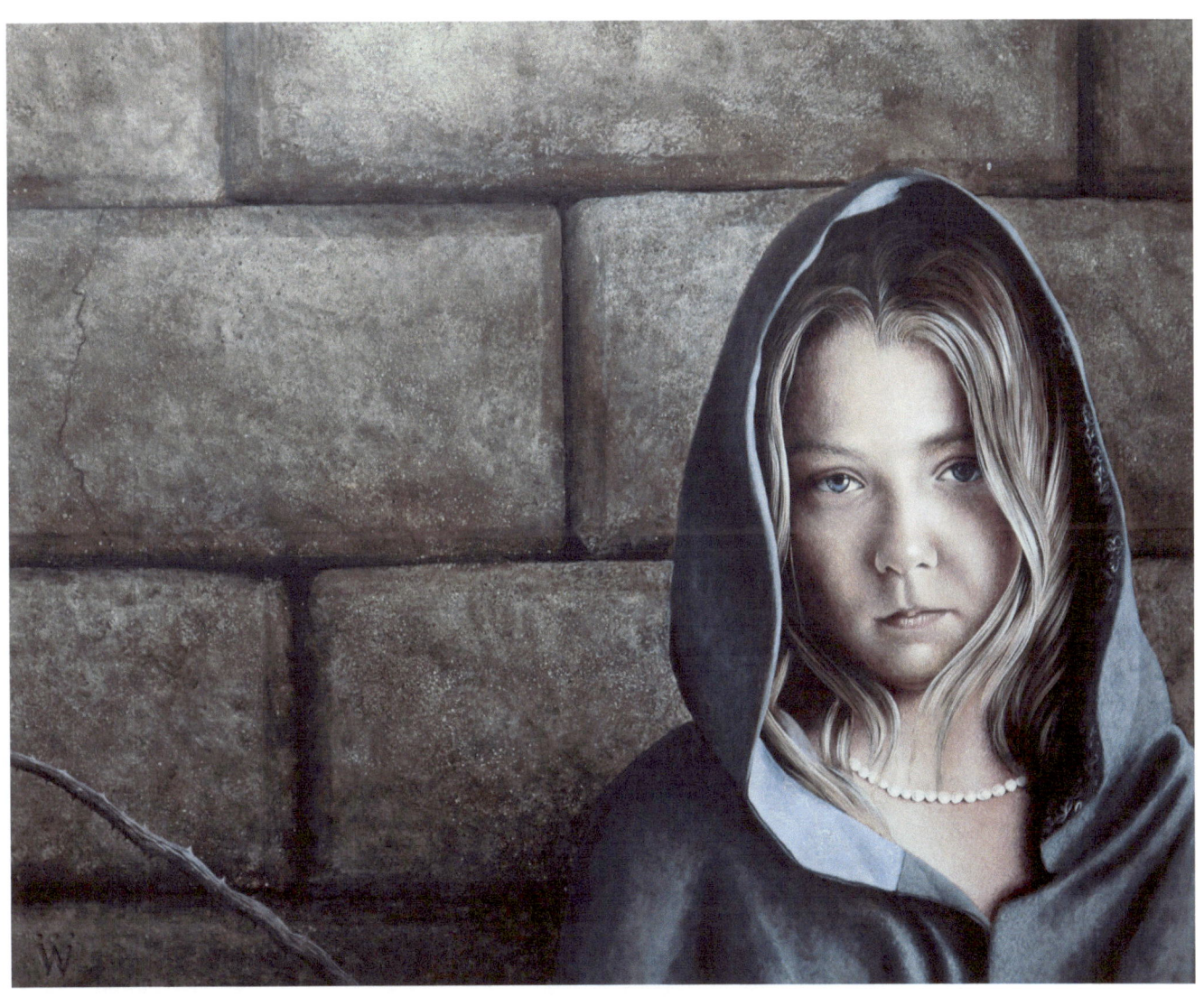

*Briar Rose*

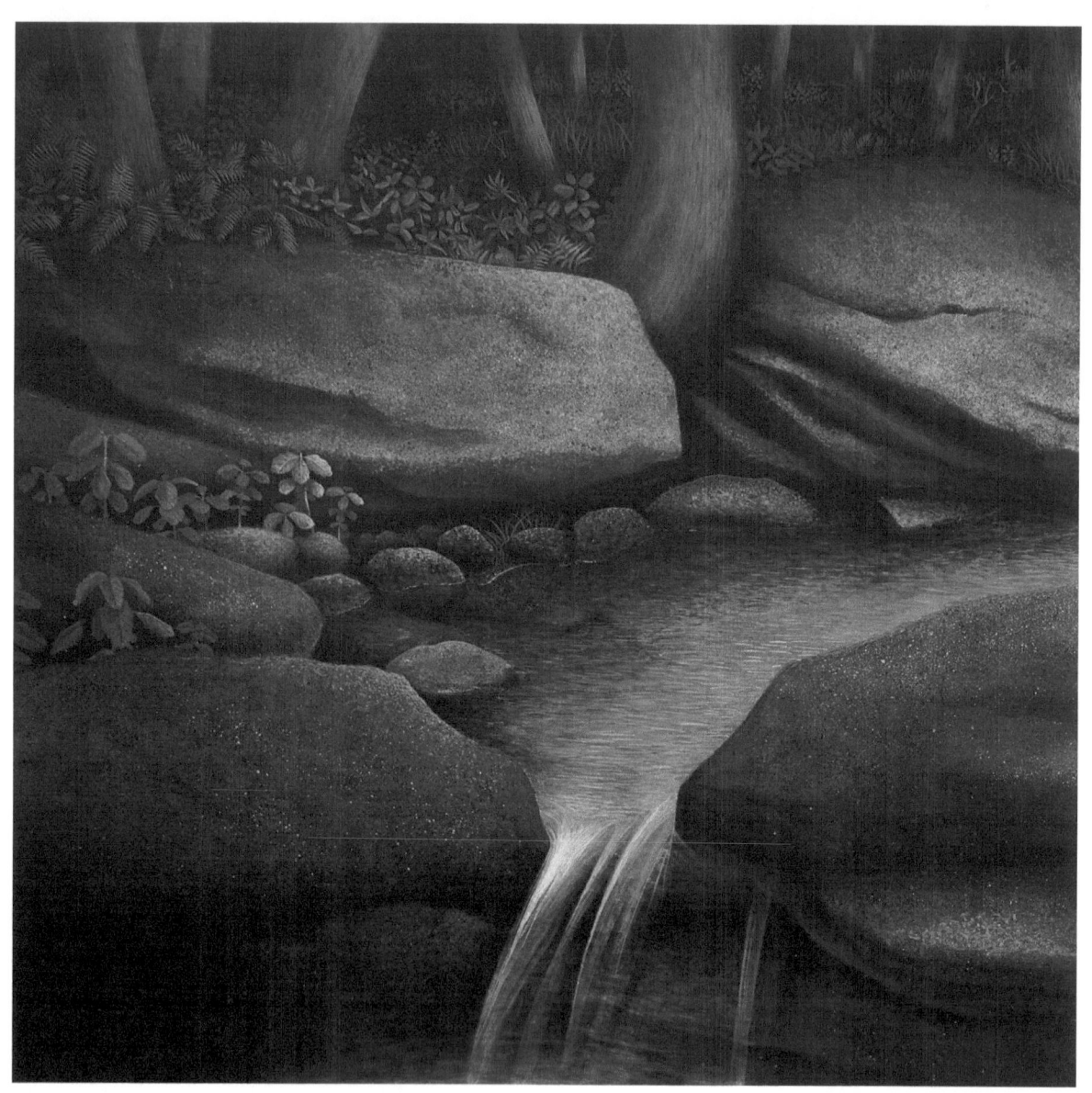

*Mermaid*

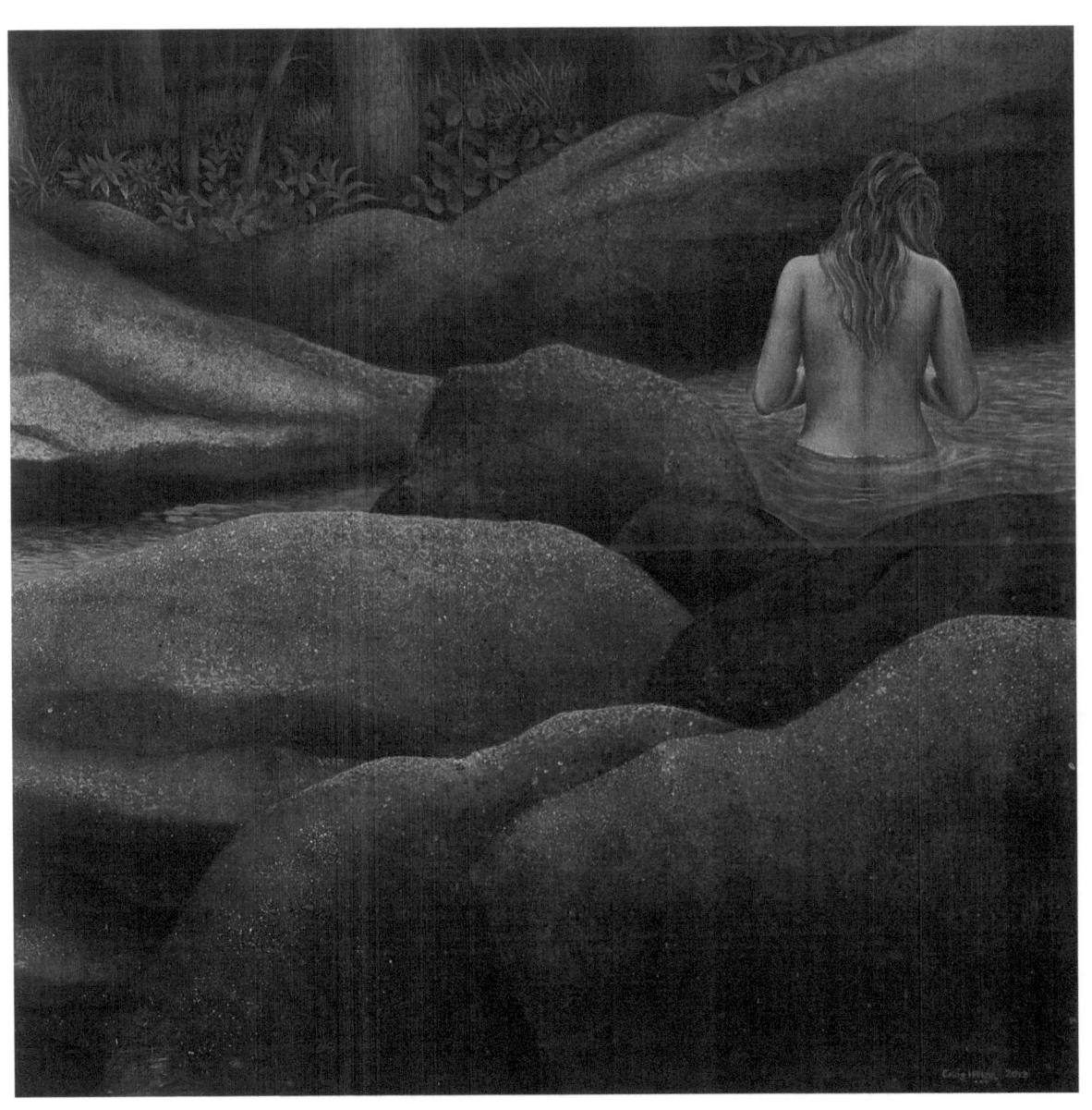

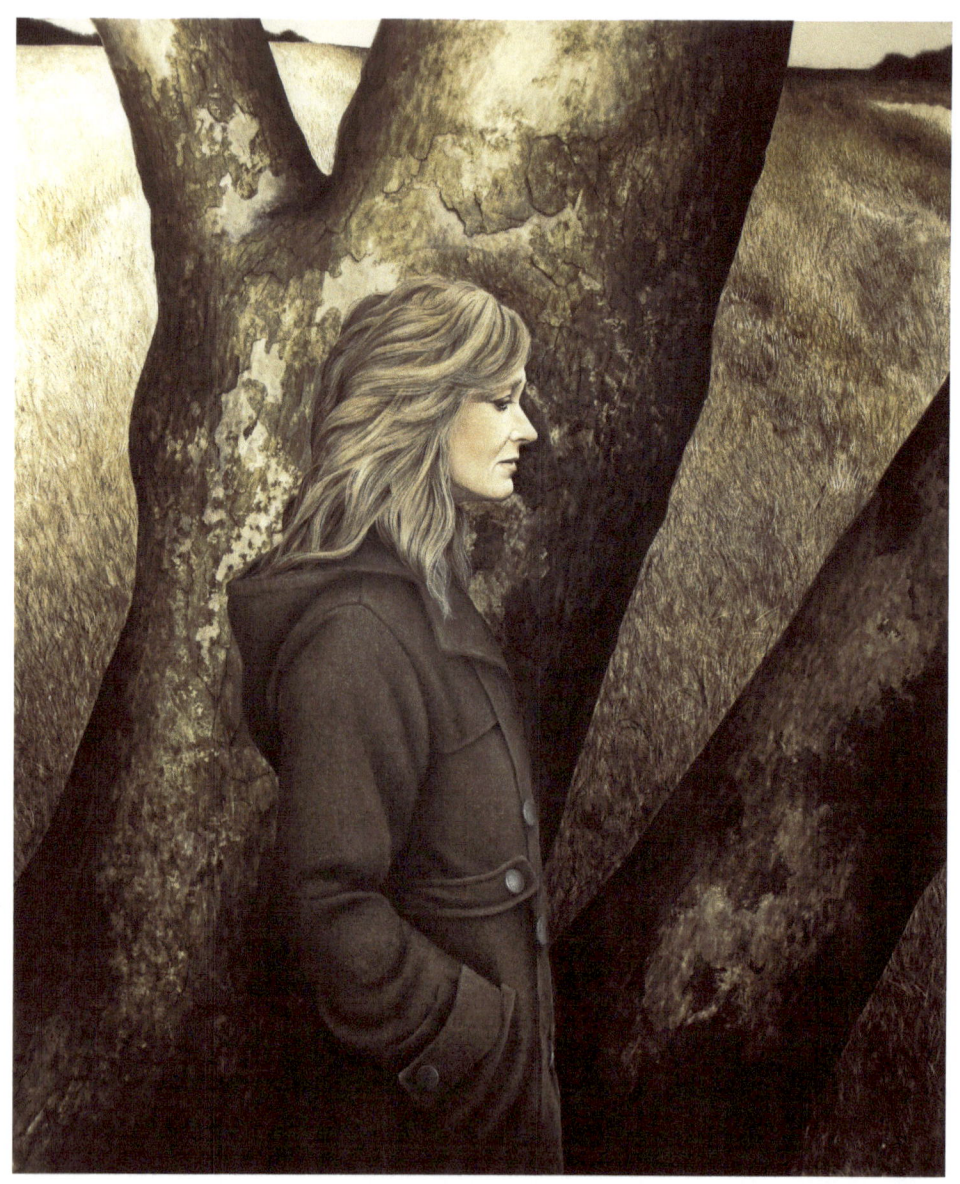

*Ides of March*

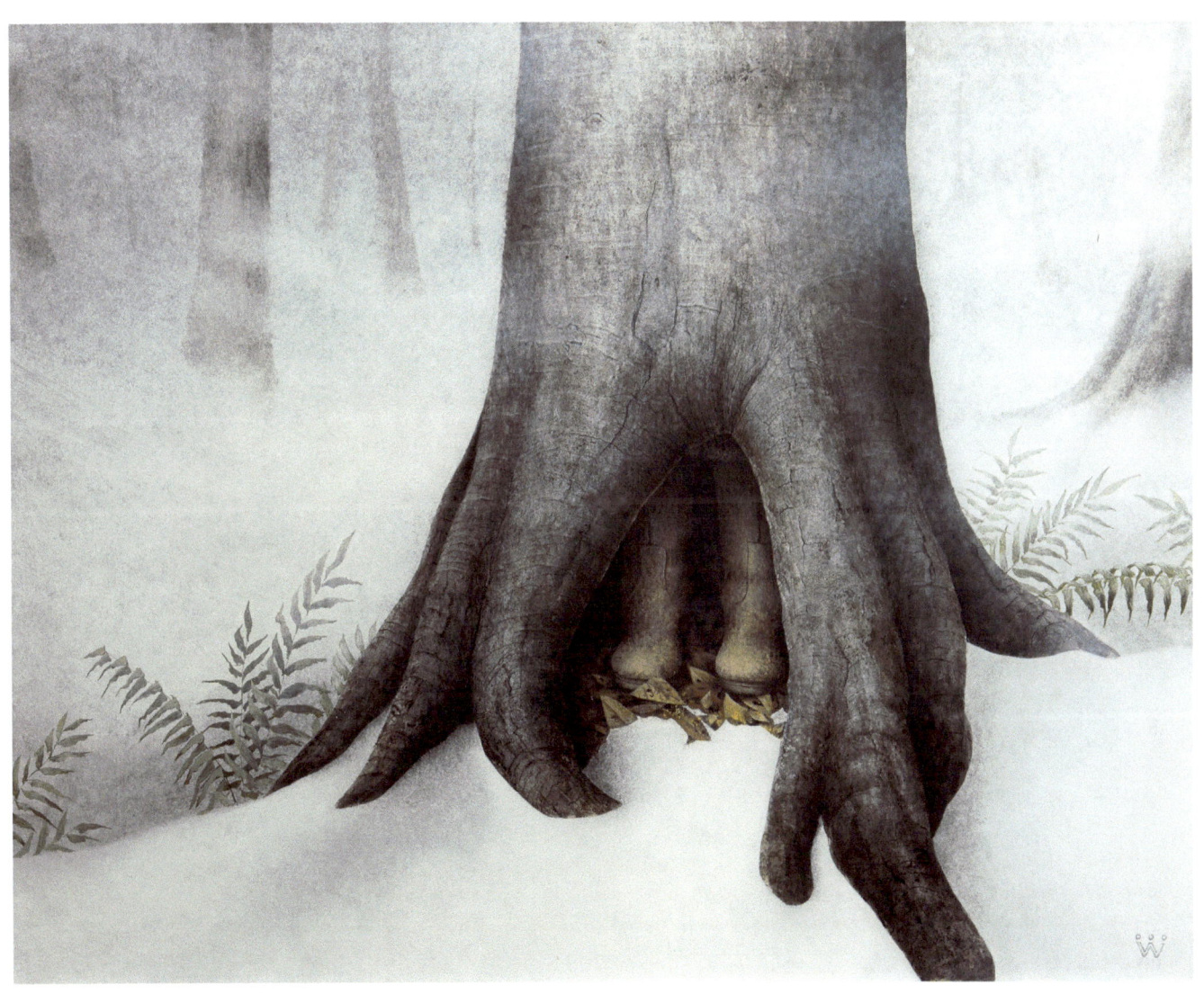

*Wood Wife*

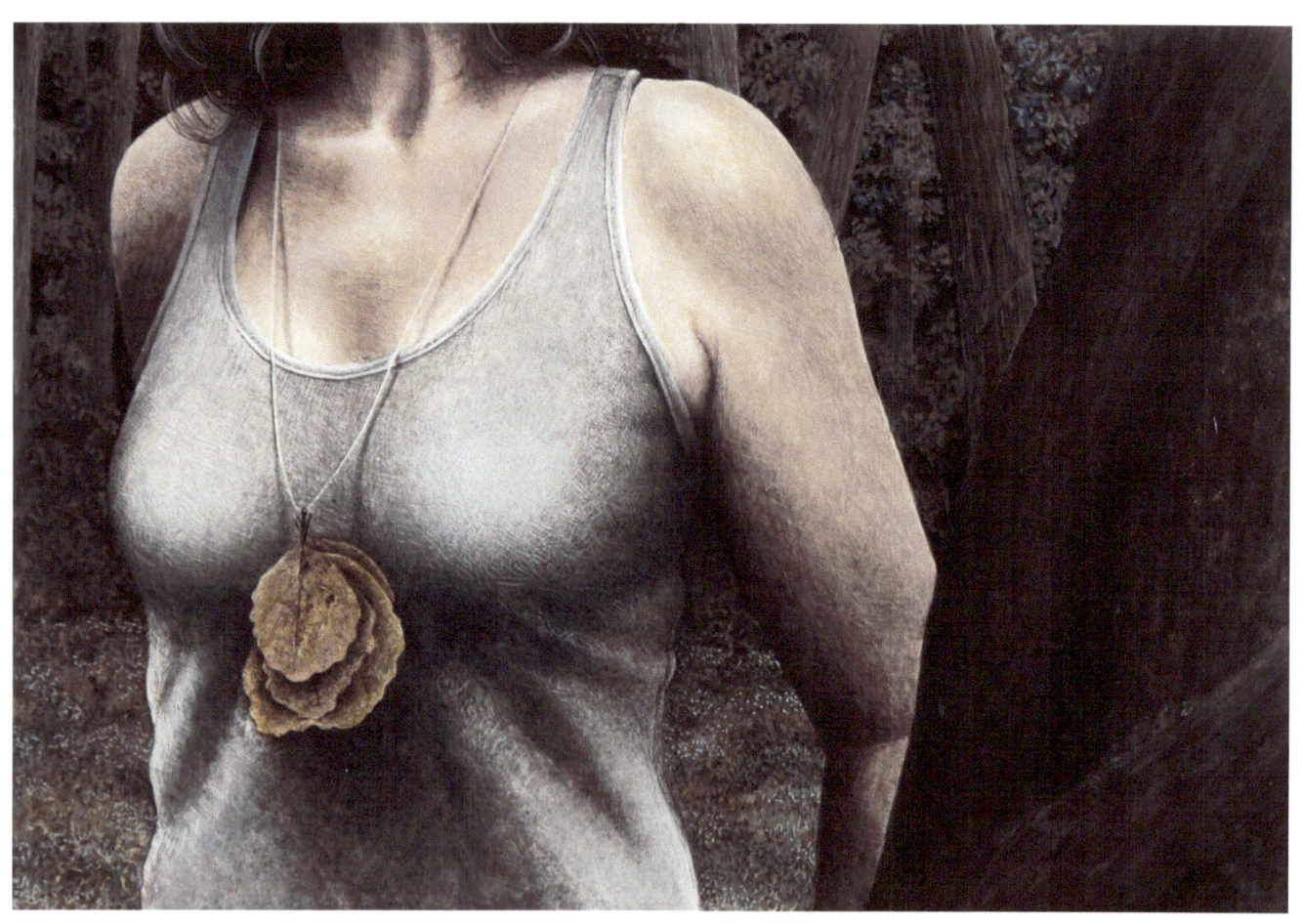

*Witch Hazel*

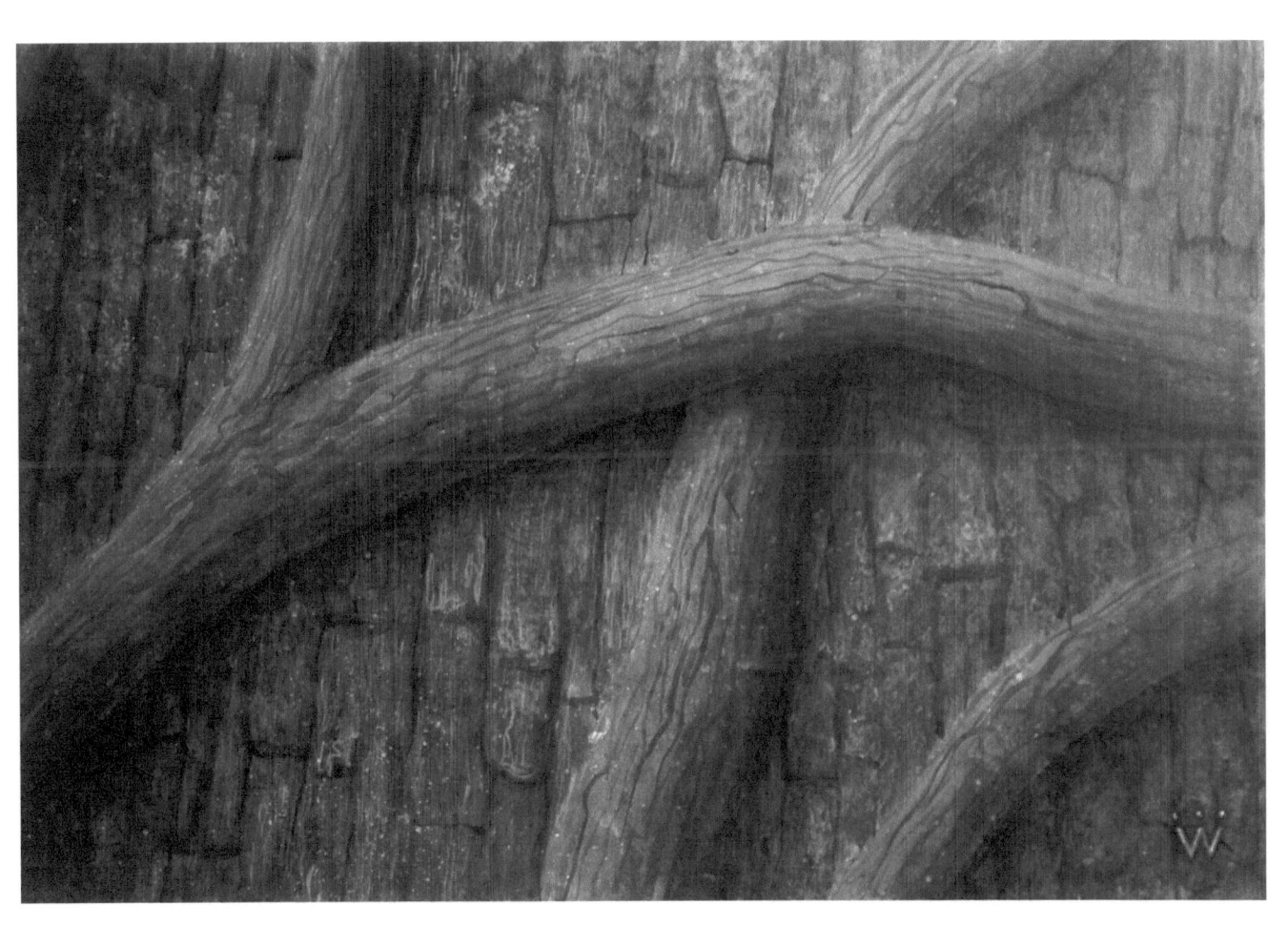

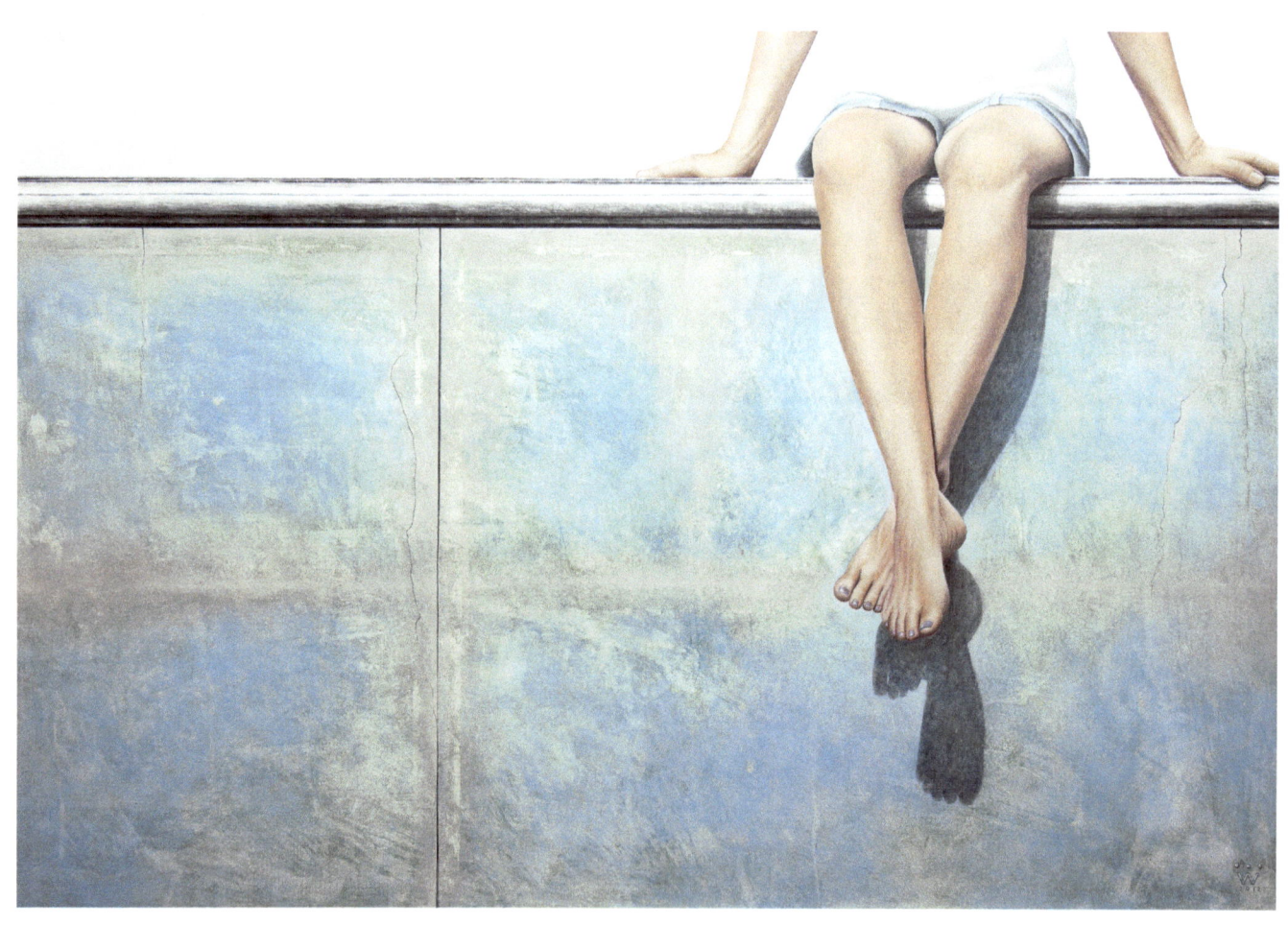

*Midsummer Madness*

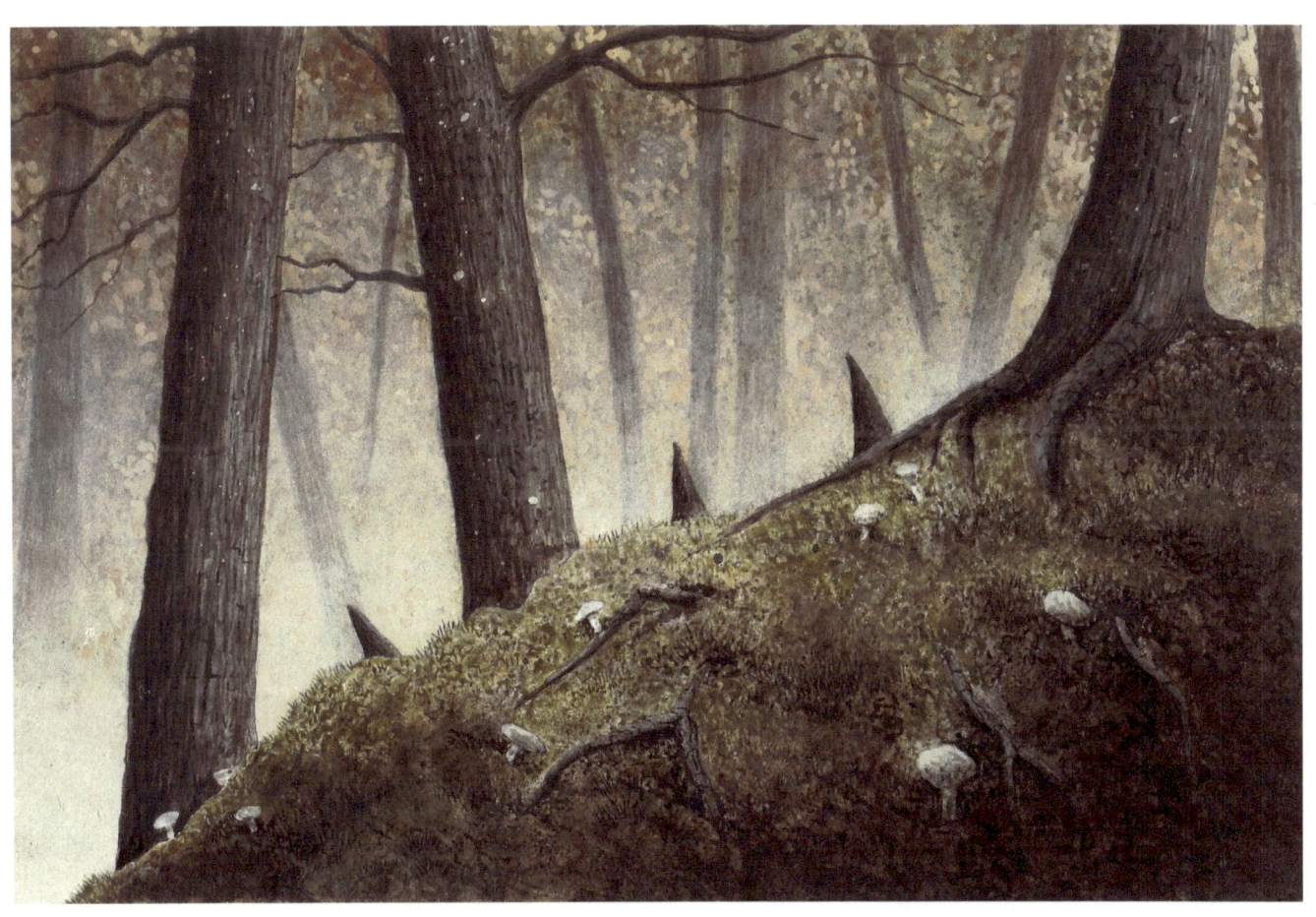

*Robin's Men*

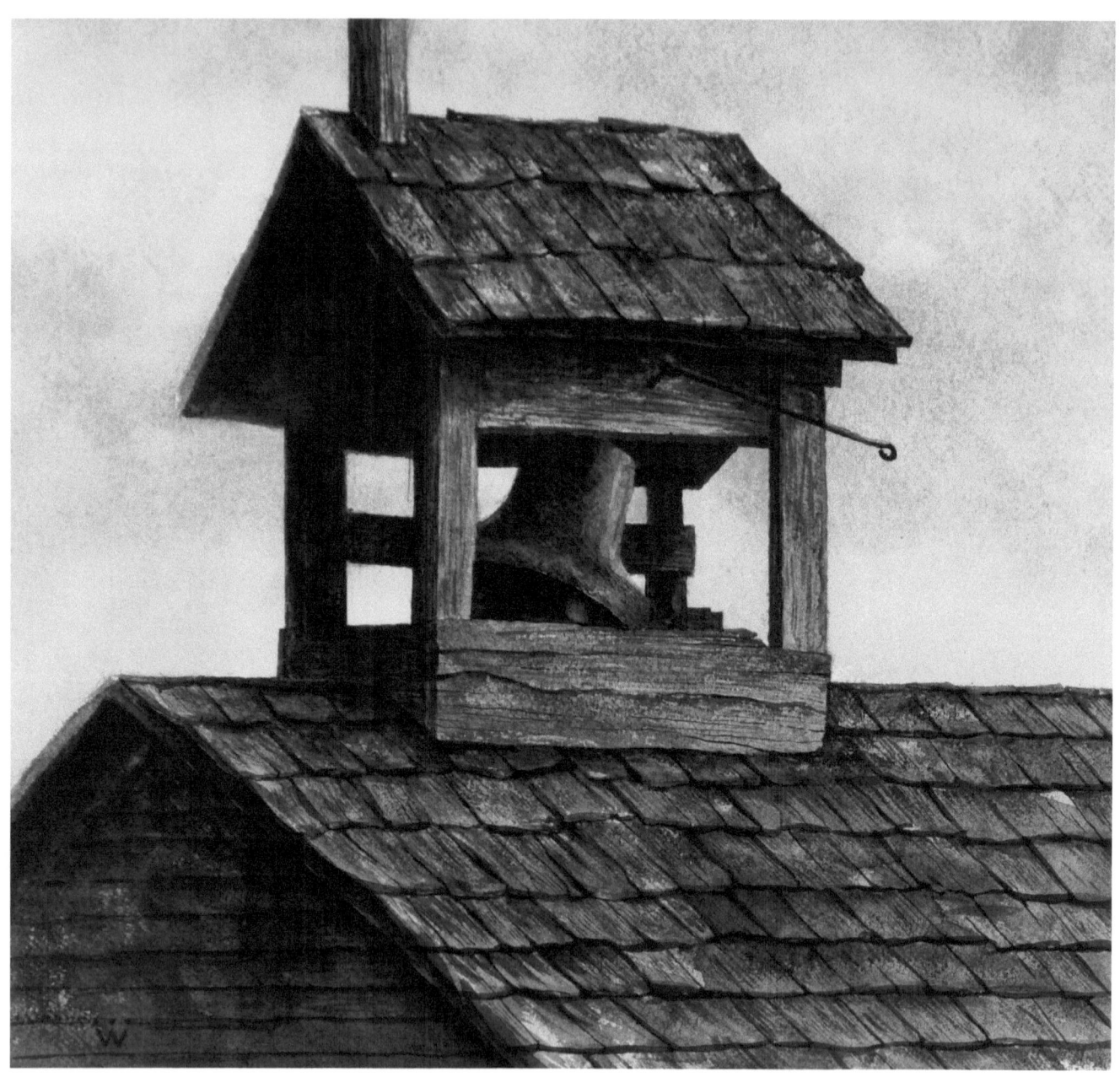

*Troll Bell*

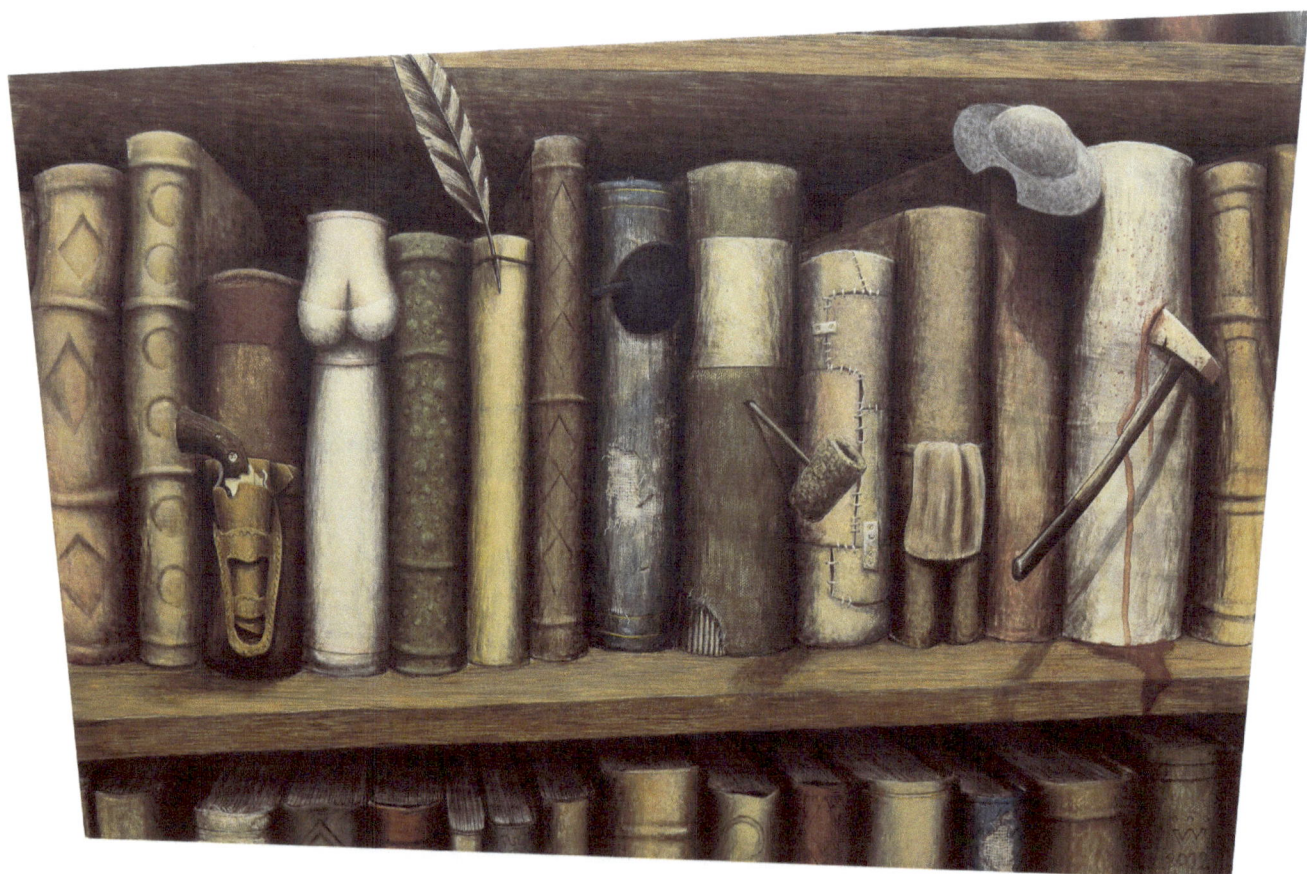

*Bibliomania*

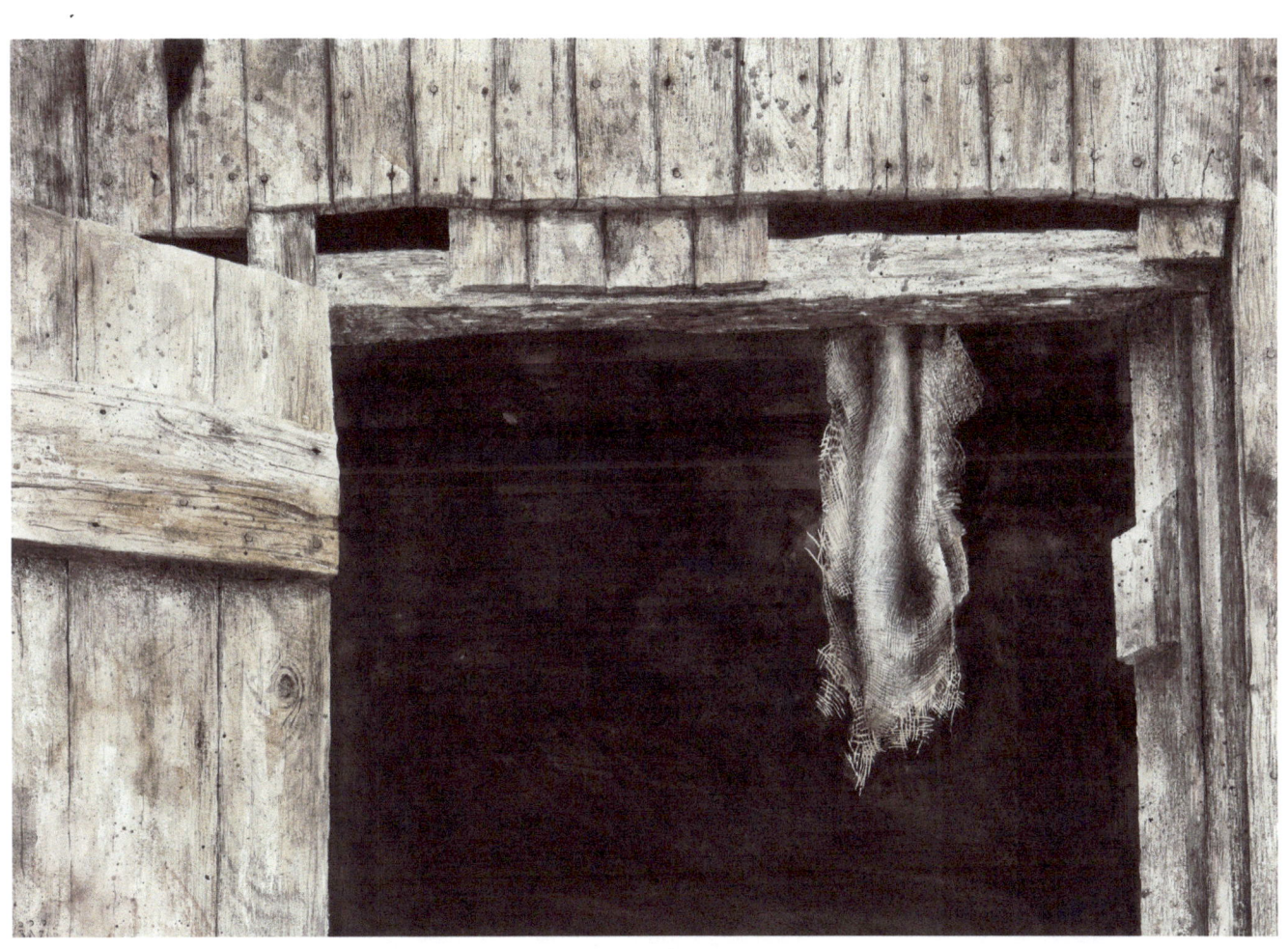

*Hessian*

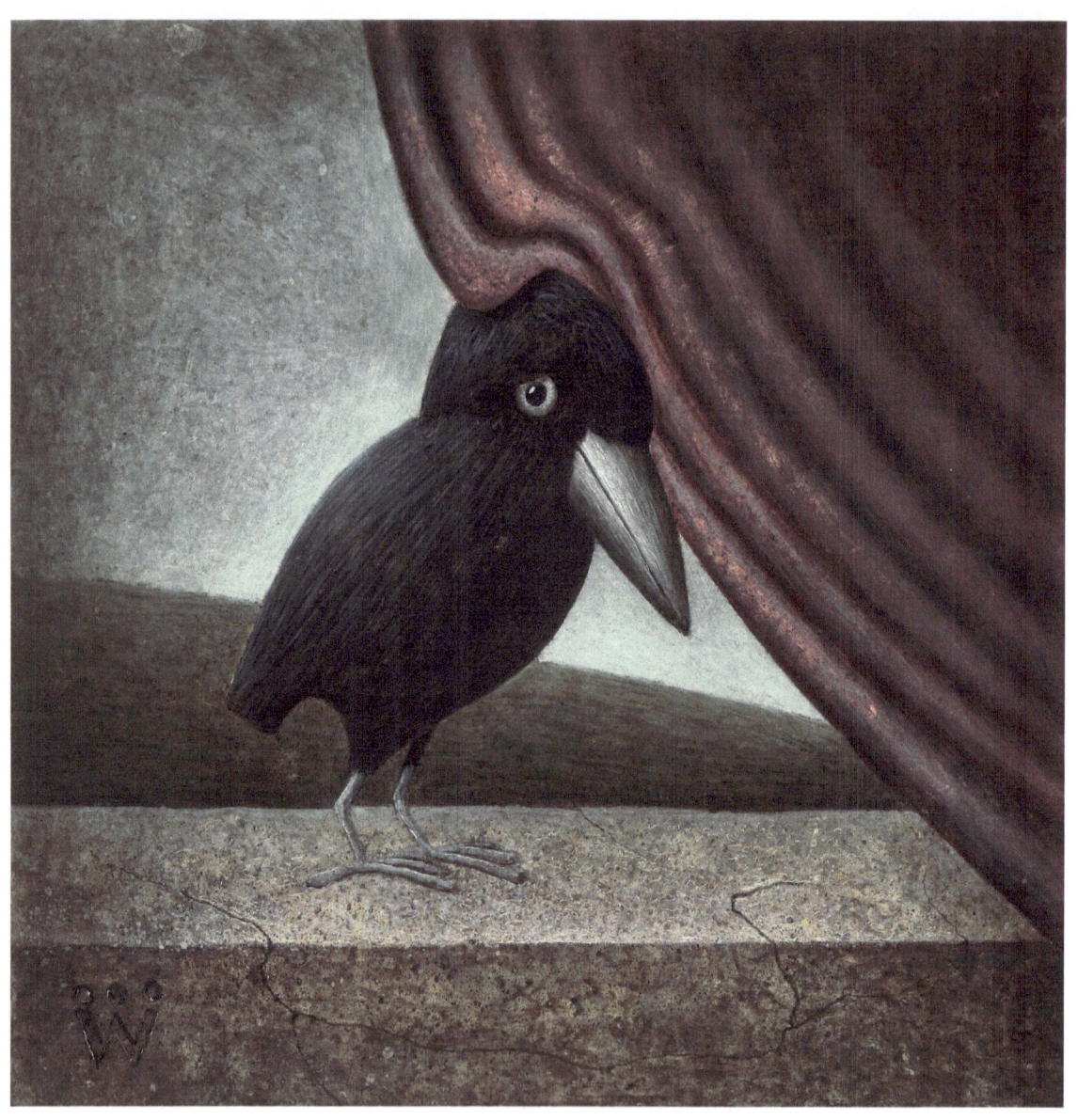

*Portrait of a Crow*

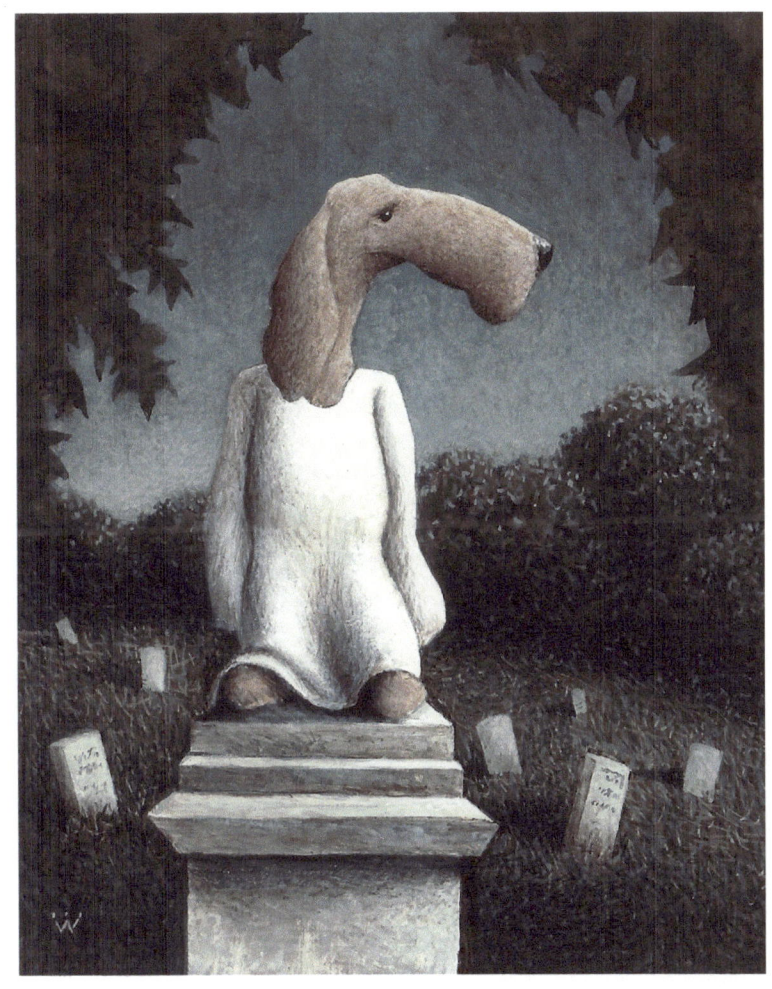

*Graveyard Dog*

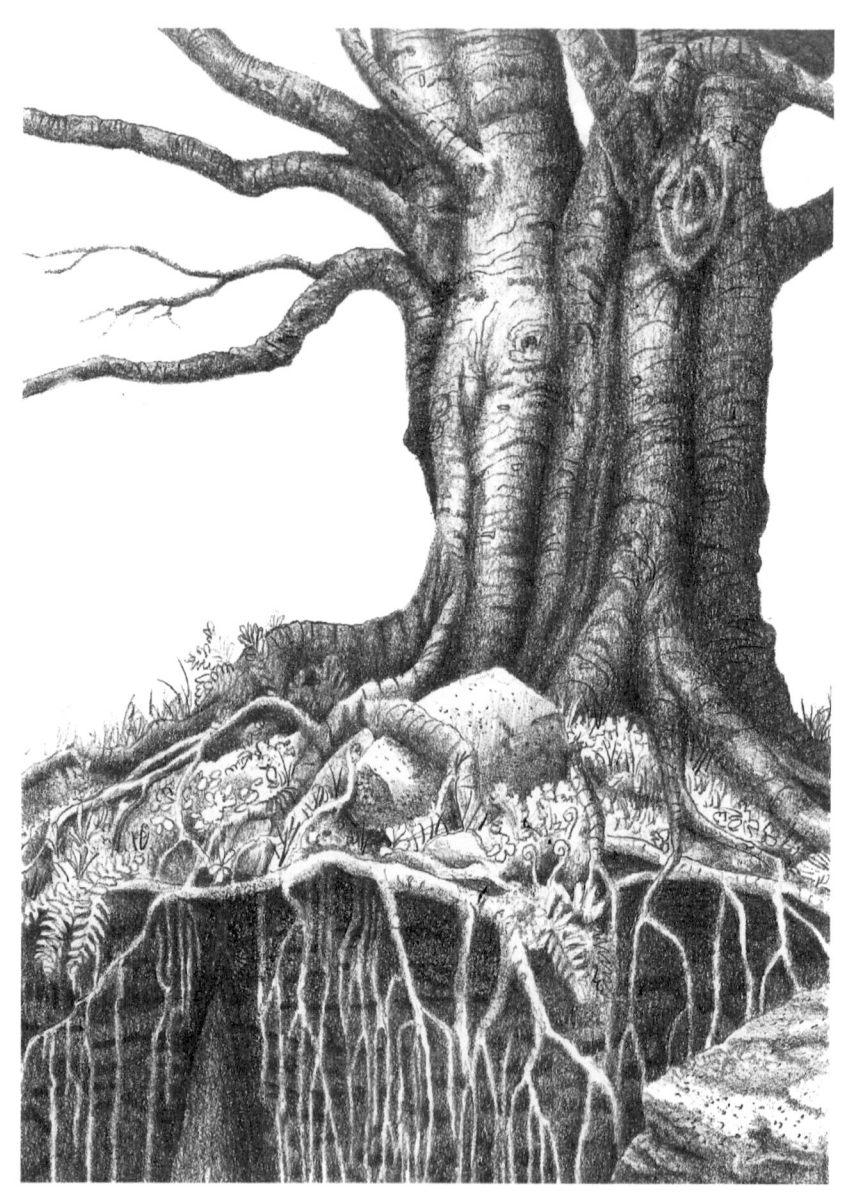

*Robin Goodfellowe*

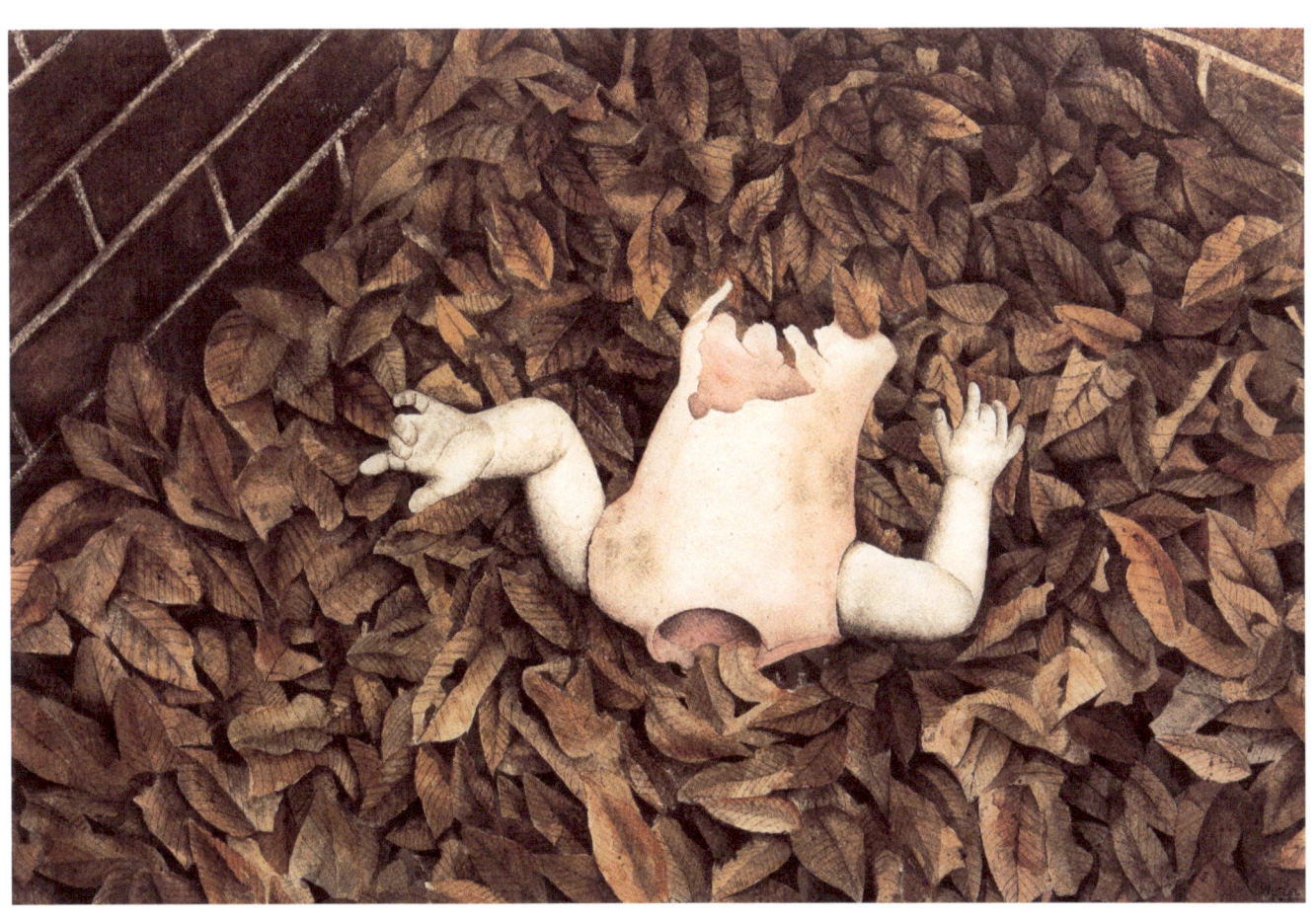

*Radio Mystery Theater*

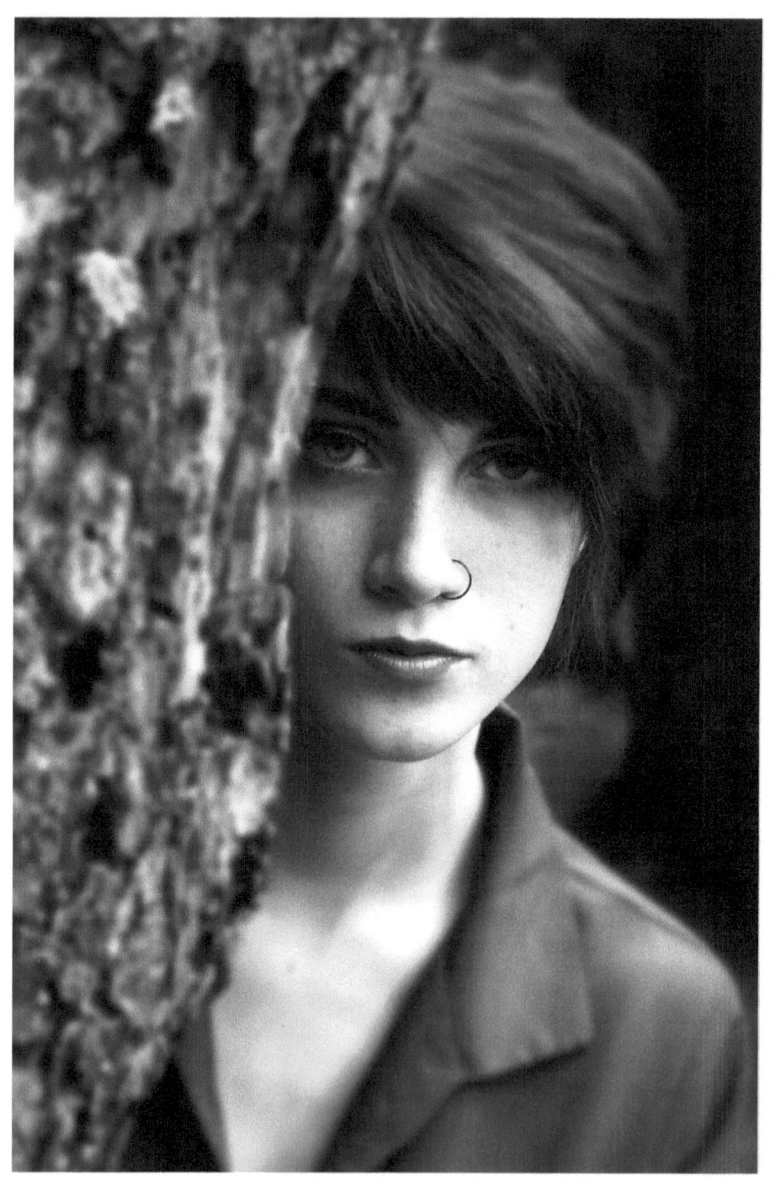

*Snow White*

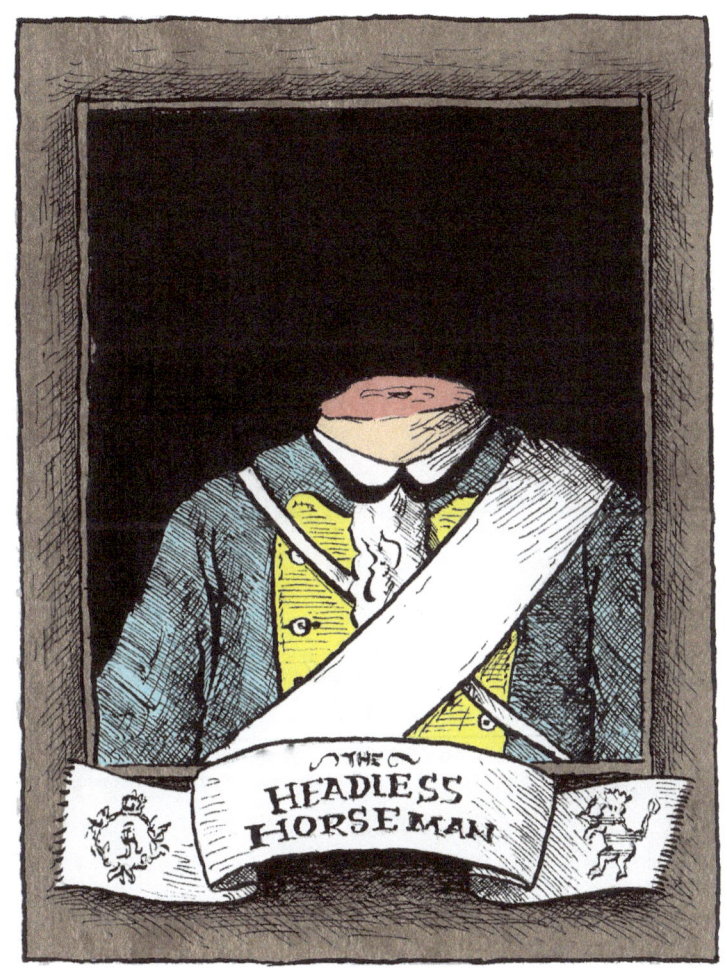

*The Headless Horseman*

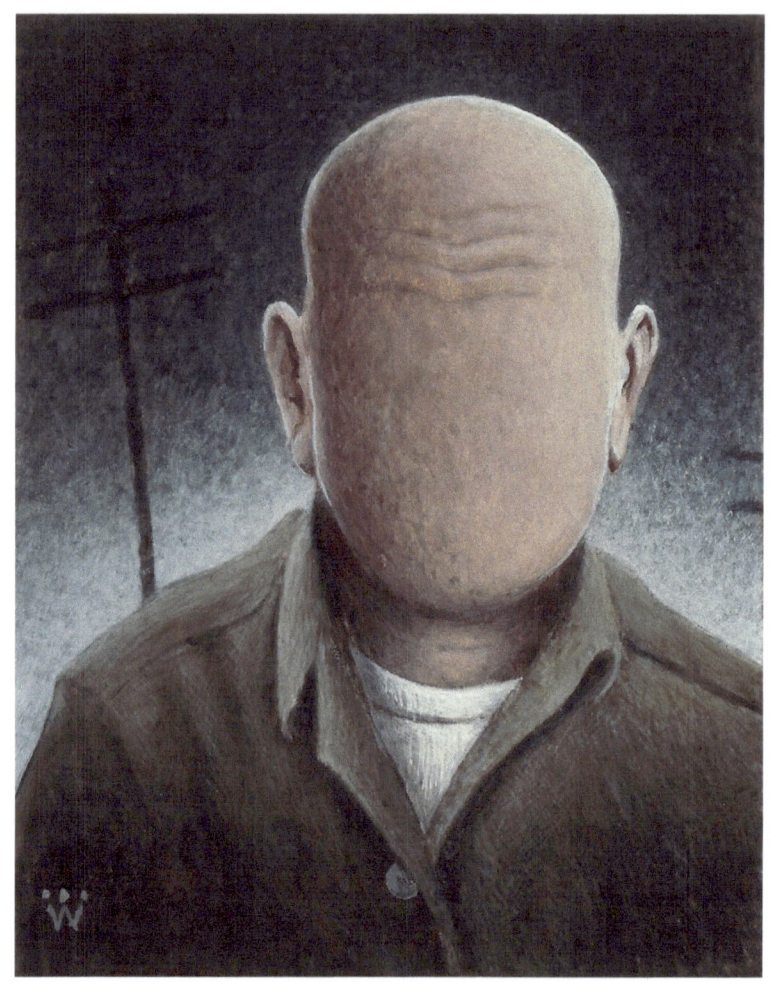

*Charlie No-face*

# Exhibition Checklist

*Briar Rose*
2013 Egg tempera on panel
29 x 23 ¼ inches
Courtesy of Princess Rapunzel

*Mermaid*
2012 Egg tempera on panel
50 x 24 ½ inches
Courtesy of Princess Rapunzel

*Ides of March*
2012 Egg tempera on panel
31 x 37 inches
Private collection

*Wood Wife*
2013 Egg tempera on panel
32 x 25 ¼ inches
Courtesy of Princess Rapunzel

*Witch Hazel*
2014 Egg tempera on panel
29 ¾ x 10 ¼ inches
Courtesy of the artist

*Midsummer Madness*
2012 Egg tempera on panel
36 ¼ x 24 ¾ inches
Courtesy of the artist

*Robin's Men*
2013 Egg tempera on panel
10 x 6 ¼ inches
Private collection

*Troll Bell*
2014 Watercolor on paper
21 ½ x 10 ¼ inches
Courtesy of Princess Rapunzel

*Bibliomania*
2012 Egg tempera on panel
23 ½ x 15 ½ x 21 ¼ x13 ¼ inches
Courtesy of the artist

*Hessian*
2014 Watercolor on paper
26 ½ x18 ½ inches
Private collection

*Portrait of a Crow*
2013 Egg tempera on panel
8 x 8 inches '
Private collection

*Graveyard Dog*
2013 Egg tempera on panel
4 x 5 inches
Courtesy of the artist

*Robin Goodfellowe*
2014 Graphite on paper
5 x 9 inches
Courtesy of the artist

*Radio Mystery*
2011 Watercolor on paper
19 x 12 ½ inches
Courtesy of the artist

*Snow White*
2014 Photograph
13 x 19 inches
Private collection

*The Headless Horseman*
2014 Ink & watercolor on paper
4 x 5 inches
Courtesy of the artist

*Charlie No-face*
2013 Egg tempera on panel
4 x 5 inches
Courtesy of the artist

*Portrait of Bear*
2012 Egg tempera on panel
13 x 16 inches
Private collection

*Potsherd*
2011 Watercolor on paper
20 x 14 ¾ inches
Private collection

*Mr. and Mrs. Jones*
2012 Egg tempera on panel
11 x 8 inches
Private collection

# Appreciation from the Artist

Most of my appreciation and one-fourth of my love go to my daughter, Madison, without whom this book would not have been made. She did the work, wrote the introduction, and ignored most of my suggestions, which is probably why it turned out so well. To Joshua Drake for his essay and for always helping me figure out just what it is that I do, something I have often wondered. To the lovely Princess Rapunzel for granting permission to print part of her speech. (I like the new bob, "Punzie.") To Matt Stewart and everyone at the Ohio Valley Regional Arts Council for making this exhibit possible. To Allison, who didn't help but asked to be included, and to Nathanael for his music selection. To Aunt Ada Sanderling for her prayers, however insincere, and to Amey Park for her suggestions and editing skills, a task analogous to Cinderella picking lentils from the hearth without any birds to help her. To my hometown of Sycamore Shadows for providing an endless parade of *comédie humaine*, to Ali Jackson for holding still, for not chomping her gum, and for ignoring the cellphone. To Hallie Delposen for deciding to buy a chicken, Curly Dowd for helping to transport the paintings and then paying for all damages incurred, Dave Pickens for photographing much of the art, Jacob and Wilhelm Grimm for providing much of the inspiration, Craig Kidd for coolest print shop in the kingdom, Hanes® for providing underwear, Jimmy and Jackie Delposen for art storage and eggs, Darrel Utt for his custom frames, and most of all, to Abigail Padden, my blue-eyed assistant at the Imaginactory. One day I will kiss you on the cheek.

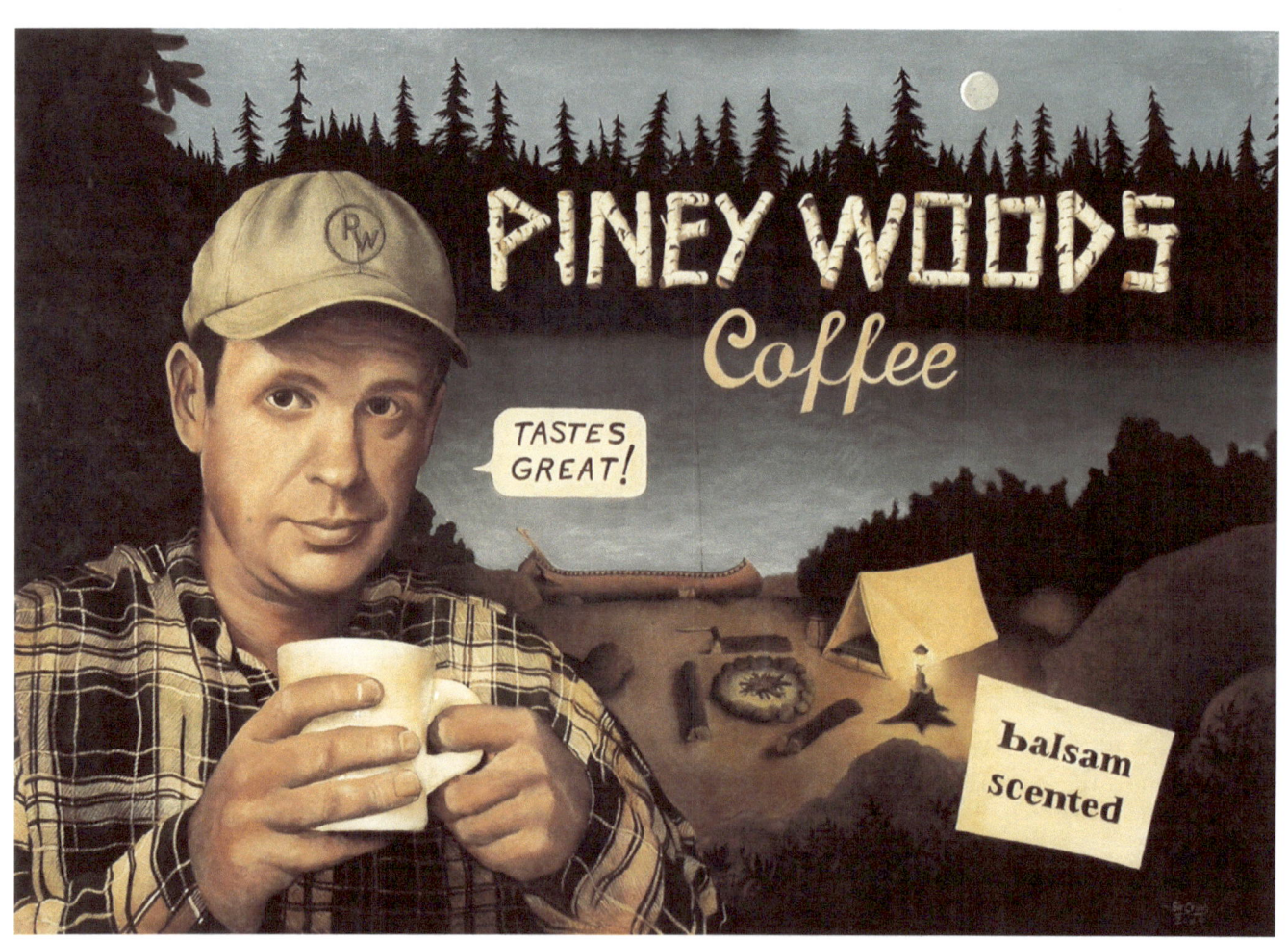

*Self-portrait*